AN OPINIONATED GUIDE

BRITISH BOUTIQUE HOTELS

Gina Jackson

Edited by
Florence Filose

HOXTON MINI PRESS

Gina reviews the most exciting and unusual hotels in Britain on her Instagram page @ginagoesto

INFORMATION IS DEAD.
LONG LIVE OPINION.

This is a simple guide, liberally sprinkled with opinion. For that we don't apologise. We know you can go online and find any information about these hotels you want, but we also know you can get a pizza with everything on it. What you want is taste. From the Scottish Highlands to the Cornish coastline, we've scoured our shores for the retreats that stand apart for their individuality, their style, their character, their design, their food, and their offer of all-out, no-holding-back luxury.

If you live in Britain, then this book is for you. If you don't, it's also for you. The recent pandemic and the ecological cost of travel has reminded us locals how much there is to savour on our doorsteps. And for those of you further afield, let us also remind you: Britain is really rather marvellous indeed. It is brimming over with breathtaking landscapes, eclectic architecture, sandy beaches, innovative fine dining and awe-inspiring art. In your hands is a guide to the best places from which to explore its cities, its coast and its culture.

Gina Jackson

THE HOTELS

THE BEST FOR...

SEASIDE ESCAPES — Take a deep breath of fresh air at Chapel House (no.7), a tranquil base from which to tour Cornwall's stunning coastline; amble through the quirky seaside shops of Deal towards the vibrant décor of The Rose (no.19); or picnic on the sand in front of Suffolk's famous multi-coloured beach huts, just a 5-minute walk away from The Swan Southwold (no.24).

PAMPERING — Need to reset? The Newt in Somerset (no.6), Beaverbrook (no.21) and Lime Wood (no.23) are all guaranteed to leave you feeling reborn, with sumptuous spas, multiple swimming pools and private treatment rooms where you'll be scrubbed and massaged from head to toe.

FINE DINING — Michelin-starred meals, bread-making workshops and chocolate tastings are all part and parcel of a stay at Hampton Manor (no.11), while The Pig near Bath (no.4) and The Pig at Combe's (no.8) '25-mile' menus serve up some of the freshest, most seasonal food around.

ART AND DESIGN — A weekend at The Fife Arms (no.12) is an immersive art experience, with a rotating selection of pieces sourced by gallerists Hauser & Wirth. Meanwhile, maximalism lovers should head to Number One Bruton (no.3) for a riot of colour and print – or, for quite the opposite, minimally chic Heckfield Place (no.17) puts on a peaceful display of the owner's own private collection.

CITY STAYS — University Arms (no.20) in Cambridge will let you discover the splendour of one of Britain's most scholarly cities, while in the heart of the English capital The Ned (no.25) hosts live music every evening and boasts more places to dine than you can count on one hand. Just outside of the urban sprawl, The Mitre Hampton Court (no.27) offers a visit to London's quieter enclaves with Hampton Court Palace and Bushy Park on your doorstep.

GROUNDS AND GARDENS	You could easily spend an entire weekend getting lost in the grounds at The Newt in Somerset (no.6), where you'll find every variety of English apple growing and even a museum dedicated to gardening. Alternatively, Heckfield Place (no.17) has 400 acres to explore – from wild swimming in the lake to cycling around the farm – while the pretty, walled gardens at Middleton Lodge Estate (no.14) are a marvel of multicoloured flowers.
COUNTRYSIDE EXPLORING	For those looking to find themselves in the middle of nowhere for a weekend, The Royston (no.9) is in prime position for hikes through the bucolic Welsh countryside, while The Rectory Hotel (no.1) sits right on the edge of the Cotswolds Area of Outstanding Natural Beauty – and outstanding it is.
ON-SITE ACTIVITIES	From bee-keeping classes and home-pressed cider tastings at The Newt in Somerset (no.6) to cookery workshops at Thyme (no.2), clay-pigeon shooting at Beaverbrook (no.21) or yoga sessions on the beach at The Gallivant (no.16), a holiday can be the perfect time to try your hand at something new.
SPECIAL OCCASIONS	Got something to celebrate? For romantic weekends away, look no further than Foxhill Manor (no.10) for an uber-extravagant adults-only retreat. Larger parties can book out the private cottages at The Rectory Hotel (no.1), Middleton Lodge Estate (no.14) or Hampton Manor (no.11) for lavish group getaways.
FAMILIES	Children have the run of the place at Beaverbrook (no.21), where the dedicated kids' club and cinema keep smaller visitors excited all day, while younger guests are welcomed with open arms at The Painswick (no.5) and will even find their own bunk beds at The Double Red Duke (no.15) and The Mitre Hampton Court (no.27).
SWITCHING OFF	Step away from the smartphone, we're going off grid. If your definition of luxury is not being able to check your emails, head to Elmley (no.18) for a rejuvenating stay in a sumptuous shepherd's hut surrounded by marshland. The lack of TVs at Killiehuntly (no.13) on the other hand leaves you no choice but to explore its 4,000 acres of wilderness in the Scottish Highlands.

*The Lodge at Thyme (no. 2) has an array of lovely rooms,
including two botanical-themed suites.*

This page: Breakfast at Elmley (no.18)
Opposite: Deal seafront is a short walk from The Rose (no.19)

The décor at Heckfield Place (no.17) is inspired by
the natural beauty of its grounds and gardens.

1

THE RECTORY HOTEL

Laidback yet luxurious Cotswolds retreat

Crudwell, the tiny Wiltshire village in which this
honey-coloured hotel resides, may sound like the set
of a Simon Pegg film – and, truth be told, it is
somewhat sleepy. Luckily, the cosy enclaves
of The Rectory, so named because it once slept the
14 children of the local Rector, have all you need to
take a serene step back from reality for an entire weekend
(or longer). Manicured yet welcoming lawns, a secret
library complete with chessboard and open fire,
and small, thoughtful touches like homemade shortbread
in every room (which the staff happily gave us an
extra jar of when we couldn't help but ask) all add to
The Rectory's feeling of relaxed refinement.

Crudwell, Wiltshire SN16 9EP
+44 (0)1666 577194
therectoryhotel.com

ROOMS   Not much has changed since the Rector's days in terms of size: the main house still has 15 bedrooms, though we imagine the décor is now rather plusher. They're divided into Small, Medium, Big and Biggest (the hotel's impressive Master Suite, with a super-king-size four-poster). We'd recommend a Medium for the best ratio of cost to sprawling space: ask for one with a bath to make the most of the latter. For special occasions, there's also a three-bedroom cottage tucked away in the hotel's grounds, available for exclusive hire.

FOOD   The Rectory's Mediterranean-accented menu features simple dishes done well; from honey-drizzled, stuffed courgette flowers to homemade gnocchi, there's a focus on good, local produce. And their freshly made buttermilk waffles, available each morning, are almost a religious experience. In warmer months, the glass-house dining area opens up onto the gardens, so you can eat al fresco; but make sure you spend at least one evening in The Potting Shed, a short walk away, for exceptionally good British pub grub.

GROUNDS The hotel may not boast the sprawling woodlands of some of the other properties in this guide, but its two acres of meticulously maintained English country garden are more than enough for a relaxed post-dinner stroll or an afternoon spent sprawled out on the grass, book in hand. In summer, seek out the tucked-away outdoor pool; a hidden gem that almost always seems to be (blissfully) empty.

NEARBY If you're tempted to stray from the private playground of The Rectory gardens, you'll do best to visit by car; Wiltshire bus services are notoriously few and far between. Hop behind the wheel and travel five miles up the road to Malmesbury, where you can visit the stunning 12th-century Abbey and wander down the quaint-as-you'd-hope High Street.

Seek out The Rectory's outdoor pool, hidden within its charming English country garden.

2

THYME

Family-run escape inspired by nature
at every turn

Just on the edge of the Cotswolds Area of Outstanding
Natural Beauty, a collection of stone cottages and
outbuildings have been reimagined as a hushed private
hamlet set apart from the world. Described by its founder,
Caryn Hibbert, as 'a village within a village',
Thyme invites you for a weekend that feels more like
a lifestyle; whether you take a class at the cookery school,
book into a floristry workshop or redesign your home
at the hotel shop (stocked with the family's own lifestyle
brand, Bertioli by Thyme, alongside one-off antique
pieces), the hotel's ethos of slower living and
reconnection with nature will stay with you long
after you've checked out.

Southrop Manor Estate, Gloucestershire GL7 3NX
+44 (0)1367 850174
thyme.co.uk
No children or dogs permitted

ATMOSPHERE It's unusual to find a hotel of Thyme's size still so lovingly overseen by its founding family, but it's this collaborative cohesion that gives it such a cared-for air. Caryn and her father, Michael Bertioli, have spent the last two decades slowly acquiring and renovating the estate's buildings, first opening as a destination cookery school before expanding into the full-blown retreat of today. Vast industrial spaces and charming stone cottages have been mindfully reimagined to preserve a sense of their history and mirror their natural surroundings. The family's influence is everywhere, from fabrics featuring Caryn's hand-painted designs to a kitchen team led by her son Charlie, previously of renowned London restaurant Quo Vadis, and branding driven by his sister Camilla.

ROOMS 31 botanical-inspired bedrooms are scattered across the farmhouse, lodge and gardens – plus a few standalone cottages for larger groups. Our favourite is the 'Cedar of Lebanon' room, where a teal-painted four-poster looks out over its namesake: a colossal cedar tree pushing through the lawn.

GROUNDS Hop onto one of the hotel's readily offered Pashley bicycles and take a spin around the estate, passing by the home farm and kitchen gardens before stopping off at the serene Meadow Spa. Set back from the rest of the hotel among hedgerows of fresh lavender, a massage here foregoes piped-in whale noises for the sound of real birds chirping outside. Unwind in the outdoor pool or challenge your roommate to a match on the tennis court, then pedal back to your room to sneak in a nap before dinner.

FOOD In the converted Ox Barn's open-plan kitchen, Charlie Hibbert plates up seasonal dishes devised from the garden outside. Indulge in the likes of freshly made crostini topped with smashed peas and whipped ricotta or flaky sea bream with a side order of triple-cooked chips. At the Baa Bar, cocktails and nightcaps are served among plush velvet sofas and life-size, fluffy 'sheep seats', while a wander up the road into Southrop will lead you to the hotel's own village pub: The Swan.

Thyme has its own quaint pub, The Swan, in Southrop village.

Thyme's English Rose suite has French doors that lead out onto the lawn.

The dining room in the Farmhouse with views across the front garden.

This page: Thyme offer tours of its farm and kitchen garden.
Opposite: Dine on delicacies at the Ox Barn restaurant.

3

NUMBER ONE BRUTON

Colourful rooms in a stylish Somerset town

Even in a county famed for its chocolate-box market towns filled with creatives, Bruton is something of a one-off for its sheer volume of art galleries, design shops and restaurant openings. Meander down the High Street until you reach an ochre townhouse with a painted wooden door, behind which a cultured-kitsch paradise awaits. Crossing the threshold at Number One Bruton feels like finding yourself inside a life-sized dollhouse, complete with gorgeous tiny drawing room, eclectic vintage furniture and floral wallpapers by French design house Pierre Fray. Flop back on your super-king-size bed and gaze out at the town's goings-on, or amble downstairs to Osip, the hotel's own Michelin-starred restaurant.

1 High Street, Bruton, Somerset BA10 0AB
+44 (0)1749 813030
numberonebruton.com

ROOMS   Arranged around a pretty, private courtyard, Number One Bruton
          sits on the site of a medieval forge – in fact, buildings have been
          in use here ever since 1239. But fast-forward to the 21st century
          and you'll find an elegant array of accommodation, with nine
          rooms spread across the original building and 18th-century
          townhouse, plus a row of stone cottages renovated into larger
          (dog-friendly) suites.

FOOD   Just in case there were any doubts you'd arrived in Somerset,
          the plastic-wrapped biscuits usually found in hotel rooms have
          been upgraded for West Country classics including sharp
          Westcombe Cheddar and local cider. Evenings are best spent in
          the hotel's chic partner restaurant, Osip – a farm-to-table affair
          that earned its first Michelin star in 2021. Be warned, it's open to
          the general public at lunch and dinner so booking ahead is crucial.
          For breakfast, however, hotel guests have the space to themselves
          for a farmhouse feast with a twist. Expect creamy rice pudding
          with miso caramel and sugary, uber-flaky *kouign-amann* pastries.

DESIGN   In the main townhouse, Georgian elegance is modernised by
          candy-coloured eclecticism and a dedication to local craft. Roll-
          top baths, abundant contemporary art and embroidered textiles
          are offset by period features, curved walls and elm flooring.
          Room One, besides the additional space and lounge seating on
          offer, is worth booking just for its mint and rose-pink bathroom
          with hand-painted Italian tiles. The cottages have a more
          rustic feel – ancient fireplaces, exposed beams and quarry-tiled
          floors – while in the forge you'll sleep between original stone
          walls in industrial-meets-cottagecore décor.

NEARBY   Bruton has attracted a flock of tastemakers in recent years, whose
          artisan outposts now lure trendy city-dwellers on the weekends.
          A few days here can easily be spent hopping from café to boutique,
          collecting treasures along the way. Pick up a homegrown-rhubarb-
          and-custard doughnut from At the Chapel bakery, peruse the
          covetable homewares at lifestyle store Caro, then take a short walk
          out of town to the Hauser & Wirth estate: a stunning sprawl of
          galleries, gardens and the Roth Bar and Grill.

The hotel's bright yellow front door welcomes you in at the end of the High Street in this picturesque Somerset town.

4

THE PIG NEAR BATH

English eccentricity with a focus on fresh, seasonal food

The Pig's collection of boutique hotels scattered
across the south have achieved cult status among British
staycationers, and with their dedication to the most
delicious, local fare and prime countryside locations, it's
not hard to see why. Their ever-growing popularity makes
booking a night in one of their eight properties
(which include The Pig at Combe, no.8) something of
a challenge. But plan ahead and you may just snag
a stay at their Bath outpost, a Georgian manor house
nestled within 18 acres of the Mendip hills. With
its more luxuriant décor but same laidback ethos,
this Pig is one of the best in the litter.

Hunstrete, Pensford, Somerset BS39 4NS
+44 (0)1761 490490
thepighotel.com
No dogs permitted

FOOD
The Pigs describe themselves as 'restaurants with rooms' and, though said rooms are rather more spectacular than that add-on suggests, food is at the heart of this hotel. Many visitors come for lunch and dinner alone, where dishes revolve around what's currently growing in the kitchen garden or can be sourced from a 25-mile radius. Expect hearty cooking with simple quality in a greenhouse-like space that glows through golden hour. You can also dine outside, if the weather permits, where a pizza oven crisps up homemade flatbreads for light lunches. At breakfast, hotel guests can pig out (sorry) in privacy from a buffet table groaning with cheeses, hams, pastries and homemade granola.

DESIGN
A sweeping drive through fields of free-range chickens and ambling lambs leads you to the manor's front entrance, guarded by two stone hogs who seem friendly, rather than imposing; the pervading atmosphere of The Pig. Step inside and you'll find a shabby-chic rendition of times gone by: gold-framed portraits line a grand staircase, squashy armchairs are pleasingly mis-matched and a row of wellies wait for new wearers. In the bed-rooms, worn vintage rugs soften wooden floors and deep bathtubs are positioned by windows for bubble-infused views over the lawns. There are smaller 'Snug' rooms available for those looking to not completely break the bank, while two stand-alone suites in the gardens guarantee peace and quiet.

GROUNDS
A wander through The Pig's small estate is really more of a tour of what you'll later find on your plate; from the walled garden growing all manner of fruit and veg, to the chillies climbing up their stakes in the greenhouse and hens laying eggs for the morning, it's easy to step straight into the good life. If your countryside itch isn't quite scratched, the surrounding Somerset scenery invites a hike through field and fen.

NEARBY
Positioned between Bath and Bristol, you'll need to visit by car to have your pick of culture to enjoy in both cities. Closer by, Cheddar Gorge is worth scaling for its dramatic views, and smaller towns Frome and Mells both offer cobbled streets and cosy pubs.

Rooms at The Pig near Bath feel welcoming and homely,
awash with natural materials.

5

THE PAINSWICK

Palladian property with straightforward
sophistication

For residents of the picturesque town of Painswick,
this aptly named hotel is something of a local treasure.
It has long-standing roots in the community; constructed
in the 18th-century, the Grade II-listed building
was turned into a B&B in the 1950s and has been
welcoming guests under one owner or another ever since.
Taken over by Cotswolds hoteliers the Calcot Collection
in 2015, it's since transformed into an elegant,
17-bedroom property where modern furnishings meet
Arts and Crafts flourishes. With multiple sitting rooms,
games room and garden, The Painswick is particularly
family friendly and – unlike some other hotels –
welcomes guests of all ages.

Kemps Lane, Painswick, Gloucestershire GL6 6YB
+44 (0)1452 813688
thepainswick.co.uk

ATMOSPHERE   From the cordial welcome, to the simple, tastefully selected décor, a weekend at The Painswick feels like visiting a refined family home. The restaurant on the ground floor has an open kitchen and a long sharing table where you'll find kids, parents and grandparents mopping up toast and jam together in the mornings. Next door, a small evening menu of reliably tasty, brasserie-style dishes are served in an elegant dining room, while upstairs you're invited to loll back in one of the bar's vast, fire-side sofas and get into an amiable argument over a board game.

ROOMS   Ranging between 'Snug', 'Cosy' and 'Palladian', there are rooms for varied budgets and occasions here, but each features unfussy, high-quality fabrics and freshly baked chocolate-chip cookies on arrival. For extra-special weekends, book George's Suite, which has its own wood burner and a spacious stone balcony.

GROUNDS   The Painswick's small but perfectly pruned gardens really do offer the best views of the Cotswolds for a mile around. Our favourite feature is the teeny terrace, where you can enjoy breakfast on mosaiced tables below stone arches and take in glorious views over the hills while happily pretending you're in the Med (in summer, that is). Forego lunch in favour of afternoon tea on the lawn, where you'll be plied with pleasingly hefty sausage rolls alongside the usual sandwiches and scones.

NEARBY   Known as 'the Queen of the Cotswolds', the pretty town of Painswick is more than worth a meander – particularly towards its striking historic church – but if you're seeking more of a buzz, hop in the car and visit multi-coloured market town Cirencester. On foot, nearby Rococo Gardens, which have been flamboyantly kept since the 18th century, are a must-visit.

George's Suite is one of the hotel's most luxurious (and most spacious).

Palladian rooms have king-size beds and roll-top bathtubs.

The pretty town of Painswick is known as 'the Queen of the Cotswolds'.

6

THE NEWT IN SOMERSET

Bucolic eco-retreat with exceptional gardens

When it comes to taking a break from reality, you could do a lot worse than this manor house turned ecological estate with its own deer park, bee safari and cider press. Set within 30 acres of working farmland, forest and spectacularly planted garden, those looking to reconvene with nature will find themselves in horticultural heaven at The Newt. But even indoor enthusiasts can lie back in luxury thanks to the hotel's beautifully designed spa, inviting communal rooms and staff's overwhelming willingness to cater to guests' every whim. With sustainability and locality at its heart, a weekend at The Newt will leave you feeling well in the deepest sense of the word.

Hadspen, Bruton, Somerset BA7 7NG
+44 (0)1963 577777
thenewtinsomerset.com
No dogs permitted

GROUNDS

The Newt's lavish grounds seem to incorporate every period and design in gardening history. From a Baroque-style maze of apple trees, where you'll find a variety from every apple-growing English county, to a Victorian winter garden with displays of exotic ferns, to the wildlife-filled ancient woodland dense with 70-foot Hornbeams and age-old oaks, the hotel's complimentary garden tours walk you through an undulating vista of discovery. Providing you have a head for heights, don't miss the sky bridge, which winds its way through the treetops to The Newt's on-site museum, The Story of Gardening, where you can get hands on with seeds and soil or step into a new realm of world-class garden design through VR headsets.

FOOD

The Newt's eco-conscious approach extends to a menu made up almost entirely of produce grown on site or locally supplied. There's plenty to choose from when it comes to where (and when) to eat: the restaurant in the main house, The Botanical Rooms, operates with an open kitchen and seasonal menu, while vegetarians are deliciously well catered for at The Garden Café, which overlooks the kitchen garden most of its ingredients are sourced from. Prefer to picnic? Visit the hotel's farm shop and deli for an endless array of Somerset cheeses, freshly baked bread and apple juice or cider pressed on site.

ROOMS

In Hadspen House, The Newt's main building dating back to 1690, the polished, Georgian rooms feature original fireplaces, velvety sofas, carved four-poster beds and fully stocked minibars hiding within elegantly panelled sideboards. Their roll-top bathtubs are so huge you may be tempted to do a lap or two (though of course there's also the spa's impressive indoor-outdoor pool for that). The Stable Yard and newly renovated Farmyard have a cosier, more rustic feel: linen furnishings, fur throws and timber-clad walls.

NEARBY

With so much to explore, it's unlikely you'll want to leave The Newt's all-encompassing estate – but if you do find yourself with an afternoon to spend further afield, the stylish, art-filled town of Bruton is a pleasant morning's walk away.

The estate's original Stable Yard has been transformed into elegant accommodation, while the renovated Farmyard has its own pool.

7

CHAPEL HOUSE

Heavenly townhouse just off the harbour

In this brick-fronted Georgian home, facing out over
the port of Penzance, there's no such thing as a
room without a sea view. And in its gleaming interiors,
restored to minimalist perfection, you won't find a
reception desk: instead owner Susan Stuart has conceived
of an 'open house' hotel, where guests make conversation
across the serene double drawing room, and meals
are served informally, supper-club style, in her open-plan
kitchen. Sit outside on the sun-dappled terrace, where
exotic succulents and aloes thrive in the Cornish climate,
and breathe deep the sea air.

Chapel Street, Penzance, Cornwall TR18 4AQ
+44 (0)7810 020617
chapelhousepz.co.uk

ATMOSPHERE It's actually quite hard not to feel calm here. Once you've knocked at the little wooden door just off winding Chapel Street and climbed up the stone steps to be greeted by whitewashed floors, soft grey walls and soul-stirring seascapes, you'll find that many of life's troubles have been left on the mat. Susan hosts with an intuitive understanding of just how much interaction you're after: she's both happy to stay and chat about her French apricot jam recipe (trust us, you'll want to know its secret), and leave you to have the run of the place.

ROOMS Interiors at Chapel House fuse seaside serenity with mid-century mahogany, wildflower displays and original oil paintings by Cornish artists. Up the wide wooden staircase, where collections of vintage bottles on the windowsills refract the light, the main house's six double bedrooms each offer something unique, be it a wood-burning stove in Room Two or the sliding glass roof of Room Six. Across the terrace, two brightly decorated stand-alone suites offer more privacy and the option to self-cater.

FOOD Breakfast is served each day around the large wooden dining table. Susan makes it herself with utmost care, setting out jars of homemade marmalade and granola, and scrambling eggs to perfect softness. The kitchen stays open for grazing throughout the day, and you can help yourself to tea, coffee and cake. On Friday and Saturday evenings, kitchen suppers are a joyous celebration of local ingredients: get to know your fellow guests over crisp, white wine paired with freshly caught seafood, then wake up to one of the best Sunday brunches in Penzance.

NEARBY St Ives, Mousehole and Sennon Cove are all within easy driving distance, whether you fancy culture and water sports or simply stretches of white sandy beach. If you travel by train (there's a handy sleeper service from London Paddington), Penzance has its own array of arty shops and interesting restaurants, plus an outdoor, Art Deco lido, Jubilee Pool, which juts out into the sea.

*Breakfast and dinner are served informally at communal tables in
the open-plan kitchen and dining area.*

*Penzance Harbour is always bustling
with colourful boats.*

8

THE PIG AT COMBE

*Great food and grand architecture with
a mellow atmosphere*

The Pig hotels are on to a winning formula:
take a languishing, listed property in one of England's
most appealing areas and transform it into a
food-focused, easy-going retreat furnished with signature
boho elegance. Yet it's the micro-chain's ability to make
each of its hotels feel personal and passionate that prevents
them from losing their soul, even as they continue to
expand. The Pig at Combe, an ivy-clad Elizabethan manor
in the Otter Valley, is much like the group's earlier
opening near Bath (no.4) in regard to its reliably excellent
menu, shabbily opulent décor and cordial welcome,
but it's the sheer rolling romanticism of its 3,500-acre
grounds that sets it apart from its littermates.

Gittisham, Honiton, Devon EX14 3AD
+44 (0)1404 540400
thepighotel.com/at-combe
No dogs permitted

DESIGN   With soaring ceilings, arched stained-glass windows and original stone walls, the Grade I-listed house has an age-old grandeur that you might miss in other Pig outposts. But its imposing structure is softened by cosy, mismatched furnishings; assorted vintage armchairs, antique side tables and tasteful taxidermy are cheerfully jumbled as if in the home of an idiosyncratic collector. During the day, guests sprawl across the multiple drawing rooms, before retiring to the wood-panelled bar after dinner, where squashy floral sofas, gilt-edged portraits and crumpled Penguin Classics are illuminated by the open fire.

ROOMS   The Pig's 27 bedrooms are aptly named: from 'Snug Rooms' to 'Big Comfy Rooms', they do what they say on the booking form with plenty of plush furnishings to sink into and minibars stocked with Devonshire fudge and beers from a nearby brewery. There's also an assortment of private-hire cottages and open-plan suites, including our favourite, The Horsebox. Located in the old stable yard, its original cobbled flooring and stable partitions make it feel almost novelty, but the sleek, tonal décor reins in any feeling of gimmick.

FOOD   The Pigs are prized for their buzzing restaurants, and this one is no exception; its '25-mile menu' (the radius ingredients can be sourced from) attracts throngs of visitors at weekends. Happily, the East Devon coast is only 8 miles away, so you can expect plenty of fresh fish and seafood alongside county cheeses, locally reared meat and edible flowers from the hotel's three kitchen gardens. Dinners are hearty and wholesome, inspired by what's growing each day, followed by fresh, floral desserts such as raspberry and elderflower cheesecake or berry-topped brown sugar meringues.

ACTIVITIES   Bikes and wellies are both available to borrow so you can choose how to explore the grounds' expanse of paddock, meadow and woodland. The Potting Shed spa is just at the bottom of the garden, where a series of sweet, garden-themed outbuildings offer a full list of treatments. Further afield, the town of Honiton is an antiques-enthusiast's nirvana, and the fossil-filled shores of the Jurassic Coast are a short drive away.

*The Pig hotels are known and loved for their shabby-chic,
eclectic décor and laidback atmosphere.*

9

THE ROYSTON

Contemporary design meets country cosiness

On the outskirts of Llanbrynmair, a quiet village just
below Snowdonia, the surprising sight of a grand London
townhouse sticks out from the verdant pasture.
The Royston's original owner, a dairy farmer who found
fortune in the capital, modelled it after his 'gentleman's
residence' in Clapham, with large bay windows,
ornate fireplaces and geometric stained glass; all of which
are still in place. Today, it's owned by Clive Sweeting
and Rob Perham – who left Brighton in 2019, quitting
their London jobs in advertising in search of the perfect
place to open a guesthouse in the Welsh countryside.
After viewing just one property, they found it.

Llwynaire, Llanbrynmair, Powys SY19 7DX
+44 (0)1650 519228
theroystonwales.com
No children under 12 years old permitted

ATMOSPHERE   Lovingly named after Clive's father, Roy, and just as lovingly
              tended to, at The Royston, Rob and Clive have made hosting into
              a fine art – in fact, many of Rob's artworks are hung on the
              walls. Expect a warm welcome and relaxed, generous hospitality
              during your stay – from homemade chocolate-chip cookies in
              the rooms to offers to arrange fishing, kayaking or even mushroom-
              picking excursions. There are no TVs (an intentional decision to
              help guests switch off), so evenings are best spent pouring yourself
              a pre-mixed Negroni from the honesty bar and finding a spot on
              the terrace to watch the sun set over the surrounding fields.

ROOMS   The building may have been inspired by London, but these
              days the interiors feel straight out of Brighton. Abstract, modern
              canvases and neon furnishings pop against inky blue walls and
              period features, and there's a quirky ornament or a vase of freshly
              cut flowers in every direction. There's no such thing as a small
              bedroom at The Royston; rooms are divided into Large, Deluxe
              and Superior. For the best views over the Cambrian mountains,
              book one of the first-floor Superior rooms and sink into an
              armchair before the bay window.

FOOD   In the relaxed downstairs dining room, breakfast and dinner are
              simple, hearty meals clearly made with care. In the morning,
              choose from homemade granola and compote or a fry-up of local
              produce – featuring tomatoes picked from The Royston's kitchen
              garden. In the evening, tables fill up fast so it's best to book
              ahead; though if you do miss out, you can always take a fire-pit
              kit out to the garden instead.

ACTIVITIES   Hiking boots are an essential item at The Royston; plenty of
              trails start nearby and lead up into the Cambrian hills, where the
              views are so beautiful you'll never be able to do them justice
              on Instagram. If you travel by car, the glorious Welsh coastline is
              less than half an hour's drive away; stop off at Machynlleth
              en route to visit Wales' very own Museum of Modern Art.

Superior rooms have the best views
of the Cambrian mountains.

10

FOXHILL MANOR

*Sprawling mansion with the feel of
a private country pad*

Ever daydreamed of popping off to your second home
in the hills at the weekend? What about your eight-
bedroom, Grade II-listed, Arts and Crafts mansion in the
Cotswolds countryside? With its focus on privacy
(only overnight guests are allowed to peek behind its
imposing double front doors), home cinema and
a 'you-make-the-rules' approach, Foxhill Manor feels less
like a hotel and more like an immersive role-play
experience, inviting you to try out life as the only child
of a multi-millionaire. It's a pretty fun persona to embody
for the weekend; though it's best to be prepared to
snap out of character when you're handed the bill
at the end of your stay.

Farncombe Estate, Broadway, Worcestershire WR12 7LJ
+44 (0)1386 854200
foxhillmanor.com
No children under 13 years old permitted

GROUNDS   Set within Farncombe Estate's glorious greenery (also home to
            Foxhill's two sister hotels, Dormy House and The Fish), the
            Manor's surroundings offer a rambling-yet-kempt variety of cycle
            routes and walking trails through fields and woodland.
            Farncombe's altitude ensures the kind of panoramic views you
            really want from a weekend, looking out over the pretty village of
            Broadway and the picturesque patchwork landscape beyond.
            And if you manage to exhaust the estate's 400 acres, National Trust
            properties Hidcote and Snowshill Manor are a short drive away.

ROOMS   With only seven other bedrooms besides your own, the hotel's
            feeling of exclusivity extends to its serenely decorated boudoirs.
            Each is named after a different variety of tree; book into Oak
            if you're looking to go all out – a huge wooden four-poster
            and twin baths overlooking the grounds make for about as
            romantic a weekend as you can imagine. But with freestanding
            tubs and walk-in showers in every room (not to mention the
            Chestnut room's own dining table), it's hard to go far wrong.

FOOD   The lack of a formal restaurant at Foxhill means that guests
            are invited to eat wherever they fancy: the bar, the drawing room,
            the cinema, even the bath. The fully stocked larder is always at
            your disposal, and menus are eschewed in favour of a chat with
            the head chef, who will cook up whatever you desire that day
            from seasonal produce. Expect to be blown away by the likes of
            homemade pumpkin tortellini and indulgent cookie-dough
            desserts, as well as lavish breakfast boards laden with fresh
            croissants, homemade granola or a full English – it really is up
            to you.

SERVICE   Foxhill's small team will welcome you with open arms – quite
            literally. Making a point of knowing each guest by name, staff here
            feel more like exceptionally accommodating old friends. Book
            the 'Full Fox' rate and you'll get raiding privileges of the minibar
            (offering endless champagne top-ups) and lunch and dinner all
            in, including a picnic hamper in summer.

The bedrooms at Foxhill Manor are all named after trees, in homage to the surrounding woodland.

The Oak suite is one of the hotel's largest and most sumptuous, and a favourite with honeymooners.

11

HAMPTON MANOR

Dreamy escape for food lovers

As the train pulls into concrete-clad Birmingham
International station, and your map-app tells
you the bucolic country retreat you've been planning is
a 10-minute taxi ride away, you'll wonder if you've
been misled. But push through the suburbs, and on the
city's outskirts you'll find a stone entrance set back
from the road, behind which an undulating drive leads up
to this neo-gothic pile. Once the estate of former
British Prime Minister Sir Robert Peel, today Hampton
Manor is both a family-run hotel and foodie utopia.
A Michelin-starred restaurant, a micro-bakery, private
picnics and cookery workshops are just a taste of
the deliciousness on offer. Enough to whet your appetite?

Shadowbrook Lane, Hampton-in-Arden, Solihull B92 0EN
+44 (0)1675 446080
hamptonmanor.com
No dogs; no children under 12 years old permitted

FOOD   From the moment you wake to a huge breakfast packed with fresh produce, to the s'mores you'll roast over the fire pit last thing at night, expect to be plied with all manner of ambrosia during your visit. Guests are encouraged to treat a weekend at Hampton Manor as a three-day staycation where breakfasts, dinners and a wine tasting are included in the price. During the day, seasonal foodie activities range from chocolate workshops to bread-making classes, and you can take a guided tour of the walled kitchen garden. There's a wood-fired feast at Smoke on the first night, a candle-lit greenhouse in the grounds, before the top billing the following day: an evening at Peel's. In the Manor's own Michelin-starred restaurant, an exquisite six-course tasting menu presents dish after dish of edible art, washed down with a wine pairing for each course.

ROOMS   In the 15 bedrooms in the main house (there's another four on offer in a private-hire cottage for groups), William Morris wallpapers, earthy tones and modern prints make for inviting boltholes. There are some lovely small touches, including fresh coffee you can grind yourself, and bathrooms have huge tubs and natural, botanical products. The three suites all feature bay windows with views over the 45-acre estate and cosy seating areas; so you can put your feet up after a day of indulging.

ATMOSPHERE   The Hill family who now own Hampton Manor grew up running a pub, and this history of hospitality is evident in the hotel's cheerful, easy-going atmosphere. Staff will often offer a cup of tea or a bite to eat as they pass by (though you may not have much room left to accept), and you'll find stacks of games and newspapers in the comfy Parlour – where a record player awaits your next vinyl selection.

NEARBY   If you feel like you really must walk off last night's six courses, there's plenty of choice in the Warwickshire countryside – including nearby National Trust estate Baddesley Clinton for a lovely lakeside stroll.

*From its multiple restaurants to its walled kitchen garden,
Hampton Manor is dedicated to deliciousness.*

You'll find William Morris prints and fabrics throughout the house,
which was built in the height of the Arts and Crafts era.

12

THE FIFE ARMS

*A pilgrimage for art lovers in the depths
of the Highlands*

A hotel would have to be something spectacular to hold
a candle to the awe-inspiring natural landscape of the
Highlands. The Fife Arms holds a whole chandelier – one
that's actually a bespoke, contemporary art piece formed
from neon-lit glass antlers. 'Red Deer Chandelier',
created by LA-based artist Richard Jackson, is
one among many breathtaking commissions that have
been made specially for this five-star retreat in the
Cairngorms, opened by the co-founders of Hauser
& Wirth global gallery. A stay here is more like walking
through an installation, with something to marvel
at around every corner – and a bar that holds a different
whisky for each day of the year.

Mar Road, Braemar, Aberdeenshire AB35 5YN
+44 (0)1339 720200
thefifearms.com

DESIGN   Every nook, cranny, wall, ceiling and floor in The Fife Arms is
spilling over with paintings, prints, tapestries, taxidermy, antiques
and artefacts. More than 16,000 separate pieces were sourced
or designed to create this cornucopia, many of them inspired by
the unique topography of the surrounding area. In the main
dining room, the panelling has been painted by Argentinian artist
Guillermo Kuitca in an abstract interpretation of the Clunie River,
which runs past outside, while 'Ancient Quartz', a ceiling mural
by Chinese painter Zhang Enli, evokes the undulating colours of
Scottish agate above the tartan walls of the drawing room.

ROOMS   Each of the bedrooms here is a cabinet of curiosities in its own
right. Wander in wonder through labyrinthine corridors to a room
inspired by local culture, nature, history or famous former
guests. Depending on the theme, you might find the words of
a Scottish poet carved into your headboard, a treasure chest in
honour of Robert Louis Stevenson at the foot of your bed, or
the imagined accoutrements of Elsie Inglis, a pioneering Scottish
doctor and suffragist, lining the walls.

FOOD   It's hard to beat The Clunie Dining Room's Highland beef
Wellington followed by a bowl of sticky toffee pudding, but a plate
of haggis, neeps and tatties from the hotel's own pub, The Flying
Stag, is equally tempting (and there's even the option of vegetarian
haggis). A full Scottish breakfast will set you up for a day of
exploring the Cairngorms, and cream teas served in the drawing
room give you something to hurry home for. After dark, visit Art
Deco Elsa's Bar for a nightcap or choose a dram from the almost
infinite international whisky selection at Bertie's Bar.

NEARBY   In summer, the surrounding mountains provide a beatific bounty
of walks, cycles, hikes and drives, while in winter they transform
into a snow-covered skiing resort. Year round, the pretty stone
houses of Braemar are worth pottering through – even if only
to visit the sporran shop – while the grounds of nearby Balmoral
Castle are open to the public (as long as the Queen herself isn't
holidaying there).

Whether you opt for avocado on toast or a full Scottish fry-up, breakfast here is essential fuel for a day exploring Cairngorms National Park.

13

KILLIEHUNTLY

*Scandinavian style set within
wild Scottish scenery*

You'd think that a week spent in one of Scotland's national
parks would mean hiking home after a long day of admiring
lochs to snuggle up under thick tartan blankets, surrounded
by taxidermy (see: The Fife Arms, no.12). But while
Killiehuntly *is* in prime position for outdoor pursuits – it's
surrounded by the rugged beauty of the Cairngorms –
inside you'll find an incongruous slice of Nordic
minimalism. The 19th-century farmhouse and its
4,000-acre estate is now owned by Danish billionaire Anders
Holch Povlsen and his wife Anne, who (again, rather
incongruously) are using their riches to 'rewild' the
Highlands: restoring native forests, regenerating habitats
and opening this, a hotel providing luxury – just not
as you know it.

Killiehuntly, Kingussie, the Highlands PH21 1NZ
+44 (0)1540 661619
killiehuntly.scot

ATMOSPHERE   There are only four bedrooms at Killiehuntly, each named after
trees found in the surrounding woodland: Elm, Birch, Alder
and Oak. And with only hotel guests and staff allowed to cross
the threshold, you're never going to find it crowded – quite
the opposite, in fact. This, combined with unspoilt landscape as
far as the eye can see and a refreshing lack of flat-screen (or
indeed any) TVs, prompts the feeling that time has slowed down.
Make the most of your longer-than-usual evenings by selecting
a book from the library, pouring yourself a drink from the honesty
bar and finding a sheepskin rug in front of the fire.

FOOD   Thankfully, the hotel's pared-back approach doesn't extend to
the food: you'll wake up to a colourful spread of freshly squeezed
juices, homemade granola and scrambled eggs, be offered a slice
of still-warm cake each afternoon, and have the private chef invent
a new three-course meal for you every evening. Dishes like grilled
courgette and creamy goat's curd on fresh focaccia, followed
by wild venison or Scottish salmon then tangy lemon posset and
raspberries, are served around a communal table with your fellow
guests in a dinner-party atmosphere of joyful generosity. They'll
also pack you up a picnic lunch (in a stylish Nordic backpack),
to take with you as you trek through the hills.

FACILITIES   It's not about mod-cons here, so you won't find minibars or manicures. What you will find, however, is a wood-fired sauna housed
in a yurt and surrounded by ancient trees – with added outdoor,
icy plunge pool if you're really willing to embrace Danish vitality.
Bikes can be hired from the farmhouse, but our favourite way to
explore the landscape is to join a 'pony picnic'. Killiehuntly's herd
will carry you out into the depths of the Cairngorms, kindly
carrying provisions for the halfway point.

NEARBY   There are many ways to immerse yourself in nature at this hotel,
but the most literal of the lot is to go wild swimming in one of
the breathtaking nearby lochs – just make sure you pack a *very*
warm jumper for when you emerge.

Take a dip in the ice-cold, outside plunge pool or brave a wild swim in one of the nearby lochs, then curl up (and warm up) in Killiehuntly's cosy rooms.

14

MIDDLETON LODGE ESTATE

*Serene retreat with a rich family history
and even richer interiors*

Deep within 200 acres of North Yorkshire woodland lies
this honey-coloured former family home. The main house
dates back to 1780, and was in a state of disrepair when
the Allison family bought it almost two centuries later.
Current owner James Allison grew up on the estate,
which has over time evolved into this still family-run hotel,
lovingly renovated by him and his wife Rebecca – the
hotel's multi-hyphenate architect, creative director and
interior designer. The Allisons' affection for their story-filled
property is evident throughout, in thoughtful touches
and local materials that celebrate the surrounding landscape;
by the end of your stay, you'll be just as taken with it.

Kneeton Lane, Middleton Tyas, North Yorkshire DL10 6NJ
+44 (0)1325 377977
middletonlodge.co.uk

ROOMS   Middleton Lodge's 36 bedrooms are scattered across its grounds and original outbuildings; the Grade II-listed house itself is only hired out for private events. In the converted former coach house, potting sheds, dairy and rustic, red-roofed farmhouse (which can be booked for bigger groups), rooms have each been designed by Rebecca in a style that brings something of the Tuscan hills to God's Own Country. In some, stone walls and iron bedsteads contrast with luxurious soft furnishings and curated antique finds while elsewhere you'll find elegant tones of Aegean blue and exposed wooden beams. Rooms in the Dairy each have huge, tin hot tubs on their private garden terraces.

GROUNDS   The Lodge's walled kitchen gardens are densely packed with all manner of shrubs, flowers, fruits and vegetables, creating a lush labyrinth of colour and scent. Wander among the apple, fig and peach trees, explore the tucked-away alcoves or find a seat on the sweeping lawns. An outdoor, heated pool was recently added, as well as some relaxed treatment rooms offering massages, facials and pedicures with a focus on natural, organic products.

FOOD   While dining at the hotel's Coach House restaurant, it's not uncommon to spot your chef popping out of the kitchen to cut fresh herbs for the next course. The super-seasonal menu changes daily, with inventions varying from smoked mackerel and pickled strawberries served on a homemade crumpet, to smoked cod's roe cream with local asparagus and chervil butter. But no matter what 'estate to plate' delicacies you have to choose from, breakfast, lunch and dinner are each more delicious than the last.

NEARBY   You may well find yourself unwilling to leave the fairy-tale surroundings of Middleton Lodge – either during your stay or once asked to check out – but if anything can tempt you away, it's the moody magnificence of the Yorkshire Dales, just half an hour's drive from the Estate.

The gardens and décor at Middleton Lodge have a rustic, Mediterranean feel.

15

DOUBLE RED DUKE

*Converted country pub with oodles
of historic charm*

This inn may have been built in the 17th century,
but these days it caters to decidedly 21st-century tastes.
Once The Plough pub and hotel, it was relaunched in
2021 by seasoned Cotswolds hoteliers Sam and
Georgie Pearman – with a menu developed by steak
supremo Richard Sandiford, of Hawksmoor fame.
A lively pub atmosphere still prevails among squishy
sofas and crackling fires, though the Pearmans' knack for
bringing a boutique twist to their properties means
you'll find many an extravagance you wouldn't expect
from your local: a shepherd's hut in the garden where
you can book in for a massage, for one thing.

Bourton Road, Clanfield, Oxfordshire OX18 2RB
+44 (0)1367 810222
countrycreatures.com/double-red-duke

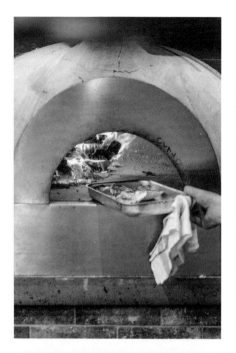

ROOMS   The Duke's range of 19 characterful rooms, from Cosy to Large, marry cheerful modern fabrics and patterned wallpapers with the sloping ceilings and exposed beams of the original building. Curated furniture champions British makers, and the pastel-tiled bathrooms have both walk-in showers and gigantic tubs. Families are welcomed with dedicated rooms and bunk beds, while the stand-alone garden rooms offer more space and solitude.

FOOD   Meat lovers rejoice. Whether you're starting with apple-glazed-bacon ribs, choosing your main from the array of steak cuts chalked up on the blackboard, or pouring gravy over a spit-roast saddle of lamb on a Sunday, there's plenty of flame-grilled succulence just waiting to fall off the bone. Vegetarians may find they don't quite feel like the target market (though there are a few options), but pescatarians will struggle to decide between melt-in-the-mouth monkfish and wood-roast scallops with a garlic crumb. Desserts are just as tempting, with classics like sticky toffee pud and ice-cream sundaes, while the highlight of breakfast is what can only be described as a posh McMuffin: loaded with bacon, sausage, egg and Ogleshield cheese.

ATMOSPHERE   Still loved by locals as a place for a weekend pint, the Double Red Duke is always buzzing with the comings and goings of country walkers and date-night diners. Find a table beneath the cheerful awnings outside, order one of the Oxfordshire ales and settle in for some people-watching.

NEARBY   The sleepy village of Clanfield in which the hotel resides is a pretty place to stroll through before dinner, popping into the 13th-century church, but it's also well situated for exploring all this area of England has to offer. In one direction, the architectural splendour and cultural pursuits of Oxford beckon, while the Cotswolds Area of Outstanding Natural Beauty offers endless walking trails in the other. Nearer by, the charming alliterative villages of Burford, Bibury and Bampton are all worth a visit – you might just recognise the last from *Downton Abbey*.

Opposite: Succulent steaks may be the stars of the Duke's menu, but dishes like roast turbot with an array of sides will please pescatarians, too.

*The Duke's stand-alone garden rooms offer extra space
and privacy with bold colours and rich textures.*

16

THE GALLIVANT

Arty rooms behind the sand dunes

A frisbee throw from Camber Sands, the largest sandy
beach in South East England, this bungalow abode
has become a firm favourite with locals and wave-craving
Londoners alike. From the outside, you'd be forgiven
for thinking it was little more than a surf café – in fact, it
was once a motel in the 60s – but step across its
weather-worn flagstones and you'll find the chicest stay
on the East Sussex coast. With driftwood-like slats on
the walls, non-naff nautical touches, and a flotsam-filled
garden, it's a popular place for beach weddings: why
fork out for flights to Malibu when there's a slice
of Californian cool just off the Channel?

New Lydd Road, Camber, East Sussex TN31 7RB
+44 (0)1797 225057
thegallivant.co.uk

*The hotel's tiny spa, in a beach hut at the end of the garden,
offers facials, massages and manicures.*

*The plant-filled restaurant has a focus on freshly caught
seafood and locally sourced ingredients.*

ROOMS Decked out in palm-leaf prints and stripy soft furnishings, the 20 bedrooms here are quirkily coastal. Choose from 'Snug', 'Baby Hampton' (for laidback luxe as the name suggests), 'Garden' or 'Luxury Garden'. The latter have French doors opening out onto the shared green space, walls lined with carefully curated books and roll-top baths divided from the rest of the room by slide-away glass doors. Breakfast, all-day elevenses, 5-o'clock wine (or kombucha) and lunch or dinner are all included in the 'Complete Gallivant' rate: quite a bit more tempting than sandy sandwiches.

FOOD Just as you'd hope when the waves are within splashing distance, The Gallivant's small, excellent restaurant places its emphasis on freshly caught seafood. Enjoy dishes like braised Hastings cuttlefish at lunch, then flake apart whole-roasted Rye Bay plaice at dinner; in fact, nearly everything on the menu here will tell you of its local provenance, right down to the selection of English wines. Breakfasts are no afterthought either, with home-made crumpets and Turkish eggs featured alongside more traditional fry-ups.

ACTIVITIES One of this seaside escape's best features is its selection of complimentary classes, designed to leave guests feeling inspired. Whether you wake up with yoga on the beach, take a guided meditation walk through the dunes, taste wines from nearby vineyards Chapel Down and Tillingham, or paddleboard down the rivers of Rye, there's much more besides sunbathing to keep you occupied. The hotel also has its own micro-spa, housed in a beach hut – if lying down and being massaged sounds much more appealing than all that activity.

NEARBY Once you've swum in the sea and made all the sandcastles you can manage, take a bus up the road to explore the hill-top, Tudor town of Rye. In its cobbled streets, you'll find antique shop after art shop, as well as the National Trust's Lamb House, former home and garden of Henry James, and Knoops: an artisan hot-chocolatiers with a whole wall of cocoa blends to choose from.

17

HECKFIELD PLACE

Down-to-earth decadence in a gigantic
Georgian mansion

From the moment you're handed a room key embossed
with your initials, you'll realise Heckfield Place does things
a little differently. Attention to detail at this Hampshire
haven goes almost unmatched: impressive in a property with
over 40 rooms. Less than an hour from London yet
surrounded by a whopping 400 acres of secluded landscape,
it took over six years to transform this 18th-century
manor into the no-expense-spared country house hotel it
is today. But among the dried flower arrangements and
original artwork – from the owner's private collection – its
warm, farmhouse finishes manage to make guests feel right
at home (except here, all the chores are done for you).

Heckfield, Hampshire RG27 0LD
+44 (0)1189 326868
heckfieldplace.com

ROOMS   With rates that range from comparatively reasonable to frankly astonishing (the Long Room, with its vaulted Georgian ceilings, private terrace overlooking the lakes and original portrait of Virginia Woolf, comes in at a jaw-dropping £5,000 per night), bedrooms here are a cornucopia of local craft. Designer Ben Thompson, a protégé of Babington House's Ilse Crawford, has turned what could have been impressive but impersonal grandeur into biophilic beauty: bringing the glorious outside in through woven textures, English oak floors and earthy tones. Plus, you'll find freshly baked biscuits in your room every day.

FOOD   Headed up by Michelin-starred chef Skye Gyngell, known for her dedication to seasonality and the zero-waste approach she pioneered at Petersham Nurseries, each of Heckfield Place's eateries offers something deliciously different. There's Hearth, with its menu centred around an impressive open fire; Marle, where dishes like wild nettle risotto and artichoke vignole are foraged from the estate's grounds or grown on its farm; and the Moon Bar – an after-dark drinking den where an enormous disco ball glitters between wood-panelled walls and cocktails are inspired by lunar phases.

ACTIVITIES   With all that acreage to explore, a morning here should be spent wandering from walled garden to woodland, picnicking on the lawn, stopping into Home Farm for a chat with one of the amiable horticulturalists, and generally pretending you're in a lavish period drama. Head back to the house in time for afternoon tea in the Glass House, then spend the rest of the day taking part in a pilates session at the spa, catching a new release in the plush film-screening room, or even wild swimming in the shimmering lake.

ATMOSPHERE   For somewhere so architecturally formidable, Heckfield Place is remarkably laidback: staff make attending to your enjoyment seem effortless, and are obviously passionate about the hotel's all-natural ethos. The restaurants offer kids' menus and smaller guests (of both the child and dog variety) will have the time of their lives larking about in the grounds.

Rooms at the back of the house overlook the estate's 400 acres of greenery.

The Long Room is Heckfield Place's most extravagant suite,
and features an original painting of Virginia Woolf.

*Everything here is inspired by nature, from the displays of dried
flowers to the seasonal menus created by Skye Gyngell.*

18

ELMLEY

Wake up in the wilderness

Sure, plenty of getaways offer 'tranquillity'.
But once you've visited Elmley, England's only national
nature reserve where guests can stay overnight, you'll
wonder if other hotels truly know the meaning
of the word. Under enormous, watercolour skies on the
remote Isle of Sheppey, glass-fronted cabins and
sumptuous shepherd's huts look out over a vast, stark
vista of all-but-untouched marsh, meadow and grassland,
above which swallows flit and buzzards soar. This
entirely unique escape offers a different kind of luxury;
room service and wifi are abandoned in favour
of the simple, restorative power of nature.

Kingshill Farm, Isle of Sheppey, Kent ME12 3RW
+44 (0)1795 664896
elmleynaturereserve.co.uk

The reserve's broad, flat marshlands make
for magical sunrises and sunsets.

ROOMS   Want to step outside your secluded wooden cabin to take a steaming outdoor shower? Or cook over a fire pit as you watch the sunset from the steps of your shepherd's hut? Perhaps you prefer waking up to the sound of birdsong from between crisp, cotton sheets in a bell tent tucked away in the woodland. Or if camping – even when the most glam of glamping – just isn't your thing, what about an elegant room in the 18th-century farmhouse, with a bathtub positioned at the end of your four-poster bed? Remarkably, all this and more awaits at Elmley.

GROUNDS With over 3,000 acres of flourishing natural landscape to admire, Elmley is dedicated to protecting England's rich biodiversity. Spend a lazy morning spotting hares race outside your window, then get out to experience it all for yourself. The mostly flat, one-way path will take you to a series of bird hides, from which you can spot an impressive list of species or simply sit and savour the silence. The first set of hides are a gentle half-hour walk away, but if you want more of a challenge, we recommend the full four-mile trek to the furthest point of the reserve, and back.

FOOD   Dinner is served in a candle-lit converted barn next to the farmhouse, with dramatic views over the marshes. There's a short menu of simple, tasty dishes made from local produce, including a drinks list featuring a sparkling English cuvée from nearby Simpsons Wine Estate. Staff are relaxed about where you enjoy your meal and will happily pack up a hamper for you to take back to your hut.

NEARBY   A 20-minute drive from Elmley lies Shellness, a strip of beach entirely made of tiny shells. Amble along this otherworldly coastline, then hop back into the car to visit The Ferry House, a pub-with-kitchen-garden where you can tuck into a particularly good Sunday lunch while looking out over Swale estuary.

Luxury bell tents nestled in Elmley's woodland let you spend a weekend immersed in 3,000 acres of glorious natural landscape.

19

THE ROSE

Creatively colourful seaside bolthole

Checking into The Rose, you might wonder if
you've mistakenly walked onto a Wes Anderson film set,
where powderpuff-pinks pop against deep tones of
velvety mustard. Colour and print are celebrated in every
corner of this former pub (even the courtyard), creating
a vibe of designed eclecticism that suits the quaint,
quirky town of Deal. Characterful sloping stairs and low
ceilings hark back to the building's historic past,
while the modern open-plan drawing room and bar invite
refined relaxation, particularly at sundown when
the shadows lengthen and a martini feels mandatory.

91 High Street, Deal, Kent CT14 6ED
+44 (0)1304 389127
therosedeal.com

HISTORY A mainstay of Deal's High Street for over 200 years, in the Victorian era The Rose was known for hosting extravagant dinners and 'entertainments'. It was taken over by John Matthews, then-owner of the Thompson & Sons brewery, in 1901 and remained a beloved boozer for over 50 years, before being sold off once more and languishing for a time as a rather run-of-the mill pub. In a satisfying twist, these days it's again owned by a descendant of the Thompson family (Matthews' great grandson, Christopher Hicks and his partner, Alex Bagner, to be precise), who reopened its doors to great acclaim in 2018.

ROOMS Each of the hotel's eight bedrooms is kitted out in its own unique flurry of colour and pattern. Choose a size from Small to Large and a view overlooking either the street or the gardens, then open a book in a fringed yellow armchair or take a soak in a jewel-toned tub. Our favourite of all is Room One, with its antique embroidered bedstead and plum-coloured walls, but Room Four, the only 'Superior' one in the house, is hard to resist with its own collection of vintage vinyl.

FOOD Breakfasts are included in every overnight stay, and guests are encouraged to order as much as they'd like from the generous menu: be it roast mushrooms with goat's curd on sourdough, or crushed avocado sprinkled with hazelnut dukkah. The main restaurant is reminiscent of a modern American diner, with wood-panelled walls and booths decked out in pea-green velvet. At dinner, you'll sit alongside locals who head to The Rose for innovative plates developed in collaboration with acclaimed chef, Nuno Mendes – crab doughnuts, anyone?

NEARBY It's likely you'll be escaping to Deal for the seaside air, so we probably don't need to tell you to take a long walk along the pebbled beach (but we can recommend it). The High Street provides plenty of interiors inspiration in the form of indie shops and cafés, and you can hire vintage bikes from The Rose then pedal off to explore Henry VIII's impressive Tudor fort, Deal Castle, which looms alongside the town.

*Room Four is The Rose's show-stopping Superior space,
with a walk-in shower and freestanding tub.*

The vibrant courtyard is a sun trap on warmer days,
and the perfect place to eat al fresco.

The pebbly expanse of Deal beach is a lovely place for a paddle in the waves.

20

UNIVERSITY ARMS

*Extravagant décor that celebrates
a scholarly city*

With its soaring stone archways and duck-egg blue
bicycles parked outside, this Cambridge hotel could easily
be mistaken for one of the city's ornate colleges: a
first impression borne out by interiors sprinkled with
varsity references. Though the space might feel
antique, and in fact the building has been a hotel in
one iteration or another for nearing two centuries,
it's actually the result of an astonishing £80-million
revamp which, from the selection of scientific tomes in
your room to the brasserie modelled on a historic
college dining hall, has been artfully designed to give you
a taste of undergraduate life... Ditch the hard work,
but keep the hedonism.

Regent Street, Cambridge CB2 1AD
+44 (0)1223 606066
universityarms.com
No dogs permitted

HISTORY   Built in 1834, University Arms is the oldest hotel in the area – but its timeline has been a little tumultuous. For 130 years, its grand, Regency façade towered over Parker's Piece, the city's great expanse of green common. In the 1960s however, a Modernist redesign left it with a rather ugly, zig-zag exterior that led straight on to a car park, and the attraction of an overnight stay here dwindled. Rescued by a collaboration between classical architect John Simpson and contemporary designer Martin Brudnizki, in 2018 it reopened its doors to reveal gleaming marble floors, restored original features and plenty of scholarly quirk – including corridors striped like the original Cambridge University tie.

ROOMS   There are now 192 bedrooms to choose from, each painted in a different hue of the University's signature blue. On the ninth floor, a series of suites named after illustrious alumni each have their own bespoke libraries curated by famed Mayfair bookshop, Heywood Hill. But if you'd rather not splash out on your reading material, book into one of the comfy, uncluttered Classic rooms and head downstairs where a dedicated 'book concierge' will show you around the communal library.

FOOD   In Parker's Tavern, the hotel restaurant, long wooden tables, red-leather seating and original stained-glass windows emblazoned with college crests might make you worry you're about to be challenged to an undergraduate drinking game; luckily the high-end British brasserie food is a little more grown up, with dishes like slow-roast Norfolk duck or asparagus and preserved lemon tart. The build-your-own sundaes on the other hand, with their huge choice of decadent toppings, reduce even the most refined guests to giddy excitement.

NEARBY   Only a 45-minute train ride from London, on weekends Cambridge teems with day-trippers exploring its 31 colleges – each more elaborately embellished than the last. Elude the crowds by hiring a punt to meander down the River Cam, where you'll float past many a gleaming spire. Then reward yourself for a day of gentle exertion with a supremely sticky Chelsea bun from Fitzbillies bakery.

*Much of the hotel's décor pays homage to the University of Cambridge,
one of the world's oldest surviving universities.*

21

BEAVERBROOK

Grand beau monde retreat with endless activities

In the former pad of Lord Beaverbrook, rooms are
named after previous guests; why wouldn't they be, when
monikers like Rudyard Kipling, H.G. Wells, Elizabeth
Taylor and Winston Churchill are on offer? From poets to
politicians, the late media mogul seemingly entertained
all of high society here in the early 20th century, and
its new owners have gone all-out in recreating the vintage
VIP experience. From the moment you pull up in front
of the neo-classical mansion, and find a flat-capped valet
waiting to whisk away your car while another gathers
up the luggage, you'll be under the (correct) impression
you're not going to have to lift a finger.

Reigate Road, Leatherhead, Surrey KT22 8QX
+44 (0)1372 571300
beaverbrook.co.uk

ROOMS   In the main house, interiors are undoubtedly old-school, with
chintzy armchairs, crystal chandeliers and decorative cornices.
Black-and-white wartime photographs (Lord Beaverbrook served
in the Cabinet during both World Wars), original artworks and
historical memorabilia keep the building's past centre stage;
though rooms also have their share of 21st-century luxuries –
flat-screen TVs, complimentary minibars and Nespresso coffee
machines. Bedrooms are also available in the separate Garden
House and Coach House, where plush pastels have been updated
for bolder colours and contemporary prints.

FOOD   Among all this preserved 1920s glamour, you might expect
rather traditional British fare; instead, you'll find the main dining
room has been converted into a high-end, Japanese grill.
Melt-in-the-mouth sushi, inventive raw fish tacos, and smoky,
glazed robata are served every evening, while a bento box menu is
available at lunch. If you're not a sashimi fan, The Garden House
Restaurant serves hearty Anglo-Italian comfort food throughout
the day in a greenhouse-like space by the walled kitchen gardens.

ACTIVITIES   Where do we start with what's on offer at Beaverbrook? You
could borrow bikes to traverse the 470-acre estate, play a game of
football, tennis, croquet or boules, try your hand at clay-pigeon
shooting or spend an afternoon fly-fishing in the ground's
trout-filled lake. And that's just the outdoor pursuits. In the main
house, an original wood-panelled home cinema (reportedly the
first to be built in Britain) screens movie marathons, the library is
lined with Lord Beaverbrook's books, history tours walk you
through the rooms' hedonistic past, and the School of Cookery
hosts chefs' masterclasses. After all that activity, wind down in the
iridescent-tiled spa, designed by contemporary artist Brian Clarke.

FAMILIES   Who says only grown-ups deserve a weekend of living in luxury?
Certainly not Beaverbrook (the hotel that is, we're unsure of the
Lord's views on the matter). From special interconnecting family
rooms to kids' menus, indoor play sessions and even a critically
acclaimed forest adventure camp on site, this hotel is one to visit
with your whole clan – even the dog.

*Framed prints and floral fabrics give Beaverbrook's interiors
plenty of vintage charm.*

The spa's three pools mean you can swim laps indoors, float past views of the Surrey Hills or let kids mess about in the outdoor splash pool.

*In the Art Deco glamour of Sir Frank's Bar, the walls
are lined with over 350 botanical paintings.*

22

THE READING ROOMS

Seaside hideaway with an exceptional breakfast

This Margate townhouse may bill itself as a B&B,
but don't be fooled; far more than kitsch quilts
and a fry-up await you behind its unassuming exterior.
Originally built as a guesthouse in the 1770s, by
the 1980s it had become ten privately let bed-sits.
Current owners Louise Oldfield and Liam Nabb,
who previously ran a design business in east London,
took over in 2007 and set about returning the
Grade II-listed building to its original purpose. Now,
just two rooms (a whole floor each) blend Georgian
extravagance with trendy stripped-back floors
and plaster-covered walls – making you feel a little
like you're in the home of a bohemian aristocrat.

31 Hawley Square, Margate, Kent CT9 1PH
+44 (0)7932 713292
thereadingroomsmargate.co.uk
No children or dogs permitted

ROOMS   With such a small selection, a room here needs to be booked
well (and by 'well' we mean months) in advance. If you do
manage to find a patch of green on the availability calendar, your
choice is between The Salon, on the first floor, and the third-floor
Attic. The Salon – once the house's grand reception room – is all
18th-century opulence, with detailed cornicing, a gilded antique
chandelier and three floor-to-ceiling windows overlooking leafy
Hawley Square. Up in the eaves, The Attic is a more rustic
loft space, with exposed lime-washed beams, artfully peeling paint
and views over the rooftops to the sea. Whichever you opt for,
a super-king-size bed will ensure you sleep easy on your decision.

FOOD   Isn't the worst part of a hotel stay having to cut short your
precious annual-leave lie in to be down for breakfast by 9am?
The Reading Rooms have seen that problem and solved it,
by making breakfast something that's delivered to your room
at any time you'd like it. And what a breakfast. Creamy scrambled
eggs, toasted sourdough, buttery croissants and fresh smoothies
are all dropped off outside your door, for you to lay out at your
own small dining table. Pull on a fluffy robe and some slippers,
and savour every mouthful.

ATMOSPHERE   With no communal spaces, you won't find a lounge or spa at
The Reading Rooms; instead expect total privacy as you hole up
in your spacious room for the weekend. Louise and Liam
are however on hand to help during your stay, with plenty of
tips on Margate's quirkiest attractions.

NEARBY   You'll be just five minutes walk from Margate's Old Town, where
specialty cafés and vintage shops abound. After rummaging
through some antique treasures, head down to the seafront to visit
the Turner Contemporary art gallery. As evening falls, pick up
a bag of fish and chips from Peter's Fish Factory and dig in while
watching the sun set over the harbour.

23

LIME WOOD

*Exquisite interior design surrounded
by peaceful forest*

Opened in 2009 by the creative minds behind The Pig
hotels (no.4 and no.8), Lime Wood is something of
a glamorous older sister to the group's other properties.
Once a hunting lodge, this truly elegant retreat has
been refined by multiple architects over the years to reach
its final form: an eclectically styled, wisteria-covered
mansion nestled in the heart of the New Forest. Industry
experts have lent a hand throughout – from polished
interiors in pastel tones by Susie Atkinson of Soho House
fame, to Italian comfort food directed by Angela
Hartnett and Luke Holder. Expect almost unparalleled
peace and thoughtful touches; starting with fresh summer
strawberries and shortbread in your bedroom, or
a welcome cocktail.

Beaulieu Road, Lyndhurst, Hampshire SO43 7FZ
+44 (0)2380 287177
limewoodhotel.co.uk

DESIGN   Every corner of Lime Wood is a visual feast: Palladian features straight out of a Jane Austen novel are set against vibrant patterns, floral wallpapers and polished wooden furnishings. Plump, pink sofas sit beside sea-foam-green armchairs on a mosaic floor and contemporary artworks line panelled, painted walls. Most impressive is the skylight bar at the heart of the hotel, where guests can sip drinks at the glitzy, marble-topped counter and dine on seasonal small plates under the stars.

ROOMS   High hopes for the rooms at a place so focused on design do not go disappointed: from cosy hideaways tucked away at the top of the house to generous suites complete with four-poster beds and luxuriant lounges, each room has its own distinctive style. Most romantic of all is the Lake Cabin, situated in total privacy away from the main house, which has something of a rustic woodland feel and a gleaming silver bathtub on its outdoor balcony overlooking the lake.

GROUNDS   With one of the UK's most beautiful national parks quite literally on your doorstep, even the indulgent interiors of Lime Wood won't be enough to tempt you away from exploring. Those visiting by car have the New Forest's full 140,000 acres of woodland at their disposal, but exploring on foot is just as easy thanks to numerous trails leading from the hotel. Start in Lime Wood's own walled garden or wander down the gravelled driveway to the little greenhouse growing fruit and veg for dinner; then stroll onwards unto the horizon – just try and be back in time for afternoon tea.

SPA   After a day spent getting (safely) lost in the forest, wind down at the hotel's Herb House Spa; three levels of indulgence offering a sauna, mud house and holistic treatments by sought-after skincare expert Sarah Chapman. Enjoy nutritious fare with a twist from the spa's dedicated café, Raw & Cured, then simply lie back and watch steam rise over the trees from the outdoor hot pool.

This page: Lime Wood's Lake Cabin is hard to beat for romantic weekends.
Opposite: Stroll past wild ponies in the surrounding New Forest.

The hotel's tranquil interiors were designed by Susie Atkinson,
the creative force behind several Soho House properties.

24

THE SWAN SOUTHWOLD

*Award-winning brewery and bedrooms
right on the beach*

You don't have to love beer to enjoy a stay in this
flamboyantly furnished hotel, steps away from Southwold's
sandy beach. But if you do, you're in for a treat.
The Adnams family set up The Swan at the same time as
establishing their brewery, which is just up the road,
in 1872, and have now added a distillery to their clutch of
local businesses. The history is hard to spot thanks to
the hotel's supremely modern reinvention by a Shoreditch-
based design studio, but some old-school touches
remain – like the hotel butlers on hand to cheerfully answer
your every question. We suggest starting with, 'Could
I have another of those delicious gin and tonics please?'

*Market Place, Southwold, Suffolk IP18 6EG
+44 (0)1502 722186
theswansouthwold.co.uk*

ROOMS   Would you rather stay in a bedroom that's 'Excellent', 'Fabulous' or 'Outstanding'? The Swan foregoes such dry customs as ranking its rooms by size, and instead asks you to choose where you're sleeping by adjective. All have contemporary seaside décor made more unusual by candy-coloured furnishings, paint-dipped four-posters and copper fittings that reference the distillery – also referenced (even more enjoyably) by a bottle of complimentary gin in the minibar. The Outstanding rooms are the biggest of the lot, with lounge areas and ludicrously large super-king-size beds.

FOOD   Of course, the beer list here is long and local – try Adnams' signature citrusy pale ale, Ghost Ship, or a Hopped Negroni made (surprisingly deliciously) with a shot of lager – but the menus in the hotel's two restaurants, The Still Room and The Tap Room, are just as perusable. The former is rather grand, with hanging still-shaped lamps and a huge copper bar, and serves seafood-focused modern British fare, including the fanciest fish supper you'll ever eat: battered monkfish and triple-cooked chips. The Tap Room meanwhile is more relaxed, with the atmosphere of a cosy modern pub, and is a nice spot for a light lunch, or a game of cards and a drink before dinner.

ACTIVITIES   Many boutique hotels offer cocktail classes – and The Swan do too – but they also go one better in their gin-making sessions where you can actually distil your own spirit, including choosing your favourite botanicals and personally labelling your bottle. Depending on your taste in tipple, take a tour of the brewery or distillery afterwards, where you'll be plied with free samples and impressed by their laudable commitment to sustainability in an industry not known for its eco-credentials.

NEARBY   From The Swan's front door, it quite literally takes two minutes to walk down to one of Suffolk's loveliest stretches of beach. Pick up some treats from one of the town's many bakeries on the way, and picnic on the sand in front of Southwold's famous rainbow-hued beach huts.

In The Swan's high-end restaurant, The Still Room, hanging bottles reference Adnams' nearby brewery and wine merchant's.

The hotel is just off Southwold's bustling marketplace, so you can watch the town's comings and goings as you sip a local ale.

25

THE NED

1920s glamour in the heart of the City

Stepping through The Ned's colossal wooden doors,
past the smartly dressed doorman, is like stepping
back in time to a far more enchanting era; here, strains of
soft jazz mingle with the clink of cocktail shakers
across a marble atrium. Left languishing for eight years
before the minds behind Soho House reimagined it,
this architectural masterpiece was originally built in 1924
to house the Midlands Bank. Now named after its
creator, Sir Edwin 'Ned' Lutyens, it reopened in 2017
as an impossibly glitzy five-star hotel enclosing
no less than 250 bedrooms, ten restaurants, and
an underground spa.

27 Poultry, the City, London EC2R 8AJ
+44 (0)2038 282000
thened.com

FOOD   Under the vaulted ceilings of the ground-floor main banking hall, an array of open-plan restaurants appear to flow into one another, allowing you to literally step between cuisines – be it fresh sushi at Kaia's long marble counter, British classics in baby-pink banquettes at Millie's Lounge, Californian smoothies and superfood salads from Malibu Kitchen, or all-American burgers, waffles and shakes among the red-leather booths of Electric Diner.

ROOMS   Upstairs, the choice of bedroom is seemingly infinite – from smaller 'Cosy' rooms with bespoke floral wallpapers and Victorian tasselled lampshades, to colossal 'Grand Heritage' suites on the Grade I-listed fifth floor. In the latter, canopied four-posters are surrounded by floor-to-ceiling, original French-polished panelling, crystal chandeliers and freestanding bathtubs at the end of the bed. There's also a selection of suites so large they feel like checking into your own (extremely select) apartment – one of which has its own 35-square-metre outdoor terrace.

FACILITIES   In The Ned's Club Spa, every kind of pampering awaits – from LED light therapy to a subterranean barbershop to a softly lit swimming pool – and a huge Moroccan hammam, clad entirely in pink marble, offers multiple hours of top-to-toe rejuvenation that will leave you feeling reborn. Live music takes place in multiple nooks throughout The Ned as evening draws in; get dressed for dinner and see what you can find.

NEARBY   It's an impressive feat to outshine even the capital's most iconic tourist attractions; but despite its super-central location, The Ned's set-up as a kind of extravagant mini-city might mean you don't step outside its doors all weekend. Though, with the Thames only a 10-minute walk away, you should stroll down to the river to admire the city skyline at least once; plus the Barbican's iconic brutalist structure and changing exhibitions are worth the 15-minute walk in the other direction.

The underground pool is a dreamy place to swim lap after lap.

The Ned's 250 glamorous bedrooms have plenty of 1920s touches.

26

TOWN HALL HOTEL

*Imposing east London architecture and
a packed events schedule*

Towering over the hustle and bustle of Cambridge Heath
Road, the impressive structure of Bethnal Green's former
town hall has been overseeing the goings-on of the
neighbourhood since 1910. Nowadays, though the Grade
II-listed building has been transformed into a sprawling
hotel, it still has the feel of a community hub. Locals stop
by for everything from immersive theatre performances
to drag bingo nights and even wolf-drawing sessions
(don't worry, the models are actually tame Lupine dogs).
Even with all this going on below, upstairs spacious
rooms and hushed corridors mean you can settle down
in total seclusion – so much so in fact that some
guests stay for years (yes, really).

8 Patriot Square, Bethnal Green, London E2 9NF
+44 (0)2078 710460
townhallhotel.com

HISTORY   Built in the heyday of Edwardian architecture, no expense was
spared by Bethnal Green Council in enlisting a team of architects
and artists to outfit the hall in ornate Baroque style. In the 1930s
an Art Deco extension was added, installing the imposing pillars,
glinting marble floor and domed skylight that today make up the
hotel's main lobby. By the mid-90s, the Council had moved to
more modern facilities and the building was left to gather dust for
over a decade until Singaporean hotelier Loh Lik Peng set about
restoring it (though it did host a few film crews over that time –
see if you can spot it in *Atonement* or *Snatch*).

ROOMS   Our favourite feature of Town Hall's 97 bedrooms is that you're
invited to bring your dog to curl up with you in every single one
of them (though it will cost you an extra £25 a night). A mainstay
on pup-friendly listicles, human guests will be just as delighted
by the rooms' décor, where original Edwardian or Art Deco
features – depending on which wing you check into – are set against
sleek contemporary furnishings. Most impressive of all are the
feature suites, including De Montfort: a soaring space in the old
Council chamber big enough to fit several houses inside it – let
alone a 20-person dining table and grand piano.

FACILITIES   As well as a stream of new events and workshops (check the
website for what's on when you visit), Town Hall encloses many
permanent play areas within its huge stone walls – from two-
Michelin-starred restaurant Da Terra to an underground pool
that featured in an episode of *Black Mirror*. On the first floor,
relaxed all-day dining is provided by the Corner Room, while in
the evenings both The Bar and The Assembly Room are abuzz
with east Londoners sipping classic cocktails.

NEARBY   After you've explored every historical inch of the hotel, head out
to experience two of east London's most renowned street markets.
On Saturdays, canal-side Broadway Market fills up with food
stalls, while Sunday mornings are for browsing through blooms
at Columbia Road Flower Market.

*The hotel lobby's huge proportions and abundance of marble
are the result of a 1930s Art Deco extension.*

Corner Room, on the first floor, attracts locals throughout the day for relaxed, bistro-style dining.

27

THE MITRE
HAMPTON COURT

Royal residence turned hip hideaway

Right on the banks of the River Thames, and steps away
from Henry VIII's favourite palace, The Mitre has
been welcoming overnight guests for more than 350 years.
Rumoured to have been built by King Charles II as
a hostel for visitors to Hampton Court, today its dark
wooden beams and sloping ceilings still make it easy
to imagine a Stuart or two swigging a pint here, even if the
rest of the interiors have been thoroughly modernised.
Its new flamboyant design feels almost cheeky combined
with the many mentions of the hotel's most famous
former neighbour – though surely even Henry wouldn't
have passed up the chance to sleep in an aquamarine
four-poster.

Hampton Court Road, East Molesey, Surrey KT8 9BN
+44 (0)2089 799988
mitrehamptoncourt.com

ROOMS   Over 100 paint colours were used in the hotel's grand revamp, creating a contemporary kaleidoscope of happily clashing colours. In the bedrooms, which are each named in reference to its royal history, hand-painted wallpapers and jewel-toned furnishings create a quirky cosiness, with many a nod to the hotel's surroundings – be it a display of vintage wooden tennis rackets (a favourite Tudor sport), or an armchair upholstered in vibrant Regatta stripes.

FOOD   Considering it's one of London's smaller boutique hotels, The Mitre has managed to fit an impressive number of gourmet dining spots into its enclaves. There's The Coppernose Bar with its casual, seafood-studded menu and views over the water, The 1665 Riverside Brasserie for high-end European comfort food on the terrace, a boat-shack bar run by rosé-masters Whispering Angel, and the glass-roofed Orangery, a private-hire space on hand for celebrations. The kitchens are overseen by Ronnie Kimbugwe, who previously spent six years with the Gordon Ramsay group, and can now be found chatting to hotel guests across the pass about his plans to install bee hives on The Mitre's roof.

ATMOSPHERE   The vibe here is one of immediate welcome: a glass of wine is handed to you on arrival and you're invited to sink down into one of the vast velvet armchairs arranged around an open fire and take a minute to recover from your journey (even if you've only come from central London). The snug library has a 1960s jukebox among its shelves of classic novels and local guidebooks, and guests are encouraged to make merry until the small hours, pouring glasses of homemade ginger liqueur from the honesty bar.

NEARBY   It would be tantamount to treason to not stop by Henry VIII's historic pad while you're on the doorstep; stroll around 500 years of garden history, get a little lost in the famous maze or take a guided tour of the Grade I-listed palace to hear centuries of salacious court secrets. Bushy Park, a huge expanse of grassland where deer roam freely, is also just across the road, while a wander down the river will provide plenty of pubs and people-watching.

The Mitre's restaurants and many of its rooms look out over the Thames.

28

REDCHURCH TOWNHOUSE

Sleek retro-styled rooms in the heart of east London

When checking into Soho House's Shoreditch outlet,
one of their few properties open to non-members,
you may find yourself wandering straight past it,
so discreet is the entrance on street-art-covered Whitby
Street. If this secretive arrival gives the feeling you're
stumbling across a stay only for those in the know – that's
because, you are. Behind Redchurch Townhouse's
unassuming exterior, five floors of appealingly retro
rooms fit right into the hotel group's reputation
for laidback, seamless service in glossy surroundings.
It's the ultimate base from which to explore one
of the capital's buzziest neighbourhoods.

25–27 Whitby Street, Shoreditch, London E1 6JU
+44 (0)2038 198180
sohohouse.com
No dogs permitted

ROOMS Less country chic (more completely chic) than other Soho House properties, bedrooms here feature jewel tones, velvet furnishings, vintage chandeliers and carefully selected mid-century pieces. In the bathrooms, fluffy robes wait by walk-in showers filled with Cowshed products, but it's the thoughtful touches that really bring these rooms to life: freshly baked chocolate cookies to welcome you; small essentials like toothpaste and hair combs just in case you forgot yours.

FOOD Underneath the hotel, on bustling Redchurch Street, you'll find Cecconi's – a trattoria with a modern twist that first opened in Mayfair in 1978 and, after joining Soho House, now serves up Italian comfort food across the world. Start your evening meal with *cicchetti* – classic sharing plates that range from truffle arancini to calamari or Puglian burrata. Huge brass vats of *cacio e pepe* or wood-fired sourdough pizzas arrive for main course; just make sure you save room for tiramisu. In the morning, the short breakfast menu includes a selection of pressed juices that will clear even the fuzziest, Aperol-spritz-induced, head.

FACILITIES Redchurch Townhouse feels more like a restaurant with rooms above it than an all-out boutique experience with endless facilities; but with so much to entice you out in the surrounding streets, it's unlikely you'll want to do much more here than recoup your energy. If your east-London escapades have left you needing more intensive rejuvenation, guests are granted access to the exclusive treatment rooms at nearby Shoreditch House – worth a visit for the celeb-spotting opportunities alone.

NEARBY In the crisscrossing lanes that surround the Townhouse, world-renowned restaurants, specialty coffee shops, vintage stores and design studios are packed in at an almost overwhelming volume. Special mentions go to Labour and Wait, for timeless utilitarian homewares, Lyle's, for chef James Lowe's truly exceptional British plates, and Spitalfields Market with its international assortment of stalls offering food, fashion and art.

The hotel's only Large room has sleek, retro-feel furnishings and a freestanding tub.

PHOTO CREDITS

Photography by *Gina Jackson* except for the images listed below.

Beaverbrook (third spread) © Susie Atkinson; Chapel House (fourth spread) © way out west photography / Alamy Stock Photo; Chapel House (second spread, above right, below right and below left, and third spread) © Chapel House; Double Red Duke (all images) © @wethefoodsnobs; Elmley (all images) © Rebecca Douglas Photography; Foxhill Manor (all images) © Foxhill Manor; Hampton Manor (first spread, second spread and third spread, right, above and below) © Fjona Hill; Heckfield Place (intro images pp.12–13, second spread, above right, below right and below left, third spread, fourth spread and fifth spread) © Heckfield Place; Killiehuntly (second spread, above left and below right, and third spread, left, above and below) © Alex Baxter & Wildland Limited; Killiehuntly (third spread, right) © Killiehuntly Farmhouse; Lime Wood (second spread, above left, third spread, left, and fourth spread, right, above and below) © Jake Eastham; Lime Wood (second spread, below right and third spread, right) © Jaime Tung; Middleton Lodge Estate (first spread, second spread and third spread, above left and right) © Cecelina Tornberg; Middleton Lodge Estate (third spread, below left) © Rebecca Allison; Number One Bruton (third spread, left) © Kym Grimshaw; Number One Bruton (third spread, right, above and below) © Emma Lewis; Redchurch Townhouse (first and fourth spreads) © Rory Gardiner; The Fife Arms (second spread) © Sim Canetty-Clarke; The Fife Arms (third spread, left) © iweta0077 / Alamy Stock Photo; The Gallivant (first spread) © The Gallivant; The Gallivant (second and third spreads) © Jan Baldwin; The Mitre Hampton Court (second spread, below left and below right, and third spread) © The Mitre Hampton Court; The Ned (all images) © The Ned; The Newt in Somerset (first spread, second spread, above left and below left, and third spread, left) © The Newt in Somerset; The Painswick (first and third spreads) © The Painswick; The Painswick (fourth spread) © Neil McAllister / Alamy Stock Photo; The Pig at Combe (first spread, second spread and third spread, right) © The Pig at Combe; The Pig near Bath (second spread, above and below right) © The Pig near Bath; The Reading Rooms (first spread) © Liam Nabb; The Reading Rooms (second spread, above right and below right) © Ollie Harrop; The Reading Rooms (second spread, below left) © The Reading Rooms; The Rectory Hotel (second spread, above and below right, and third spread, left) © Jake Eastham; The Rose (Deal seafront p.9, and first, second and third spreads) © Seth Carnill; The Rose (fourth spread) © 2ebill / Alamy Stock Photo; The Royston (all interior shots) © Rachael Smith; The Swan Southwold (all images) © James Bedford; Thyme (intro images pp.8–9, first spread, second spread, fourth spread and fifth spread) © Thyme; Thyme (third spread) © Tim Gainey / Alamy; Town Hall Hotel (first spread, second spread, above, and third spread) © Town Hall Hotel; Town Hall Hotel (second spread, below) © Justin de Souza; University Arms (all images) © University Arms.

ABOUT US

Gina Jackson is a travel blogger and photographer who, though a proud Londoner, can more often be found testing out hotel rooms all over the country. A champion of the great British staycation, she shares her personal recommendations and honest critiques on her Instagram @ginagoesto. When she's not gallivanting around between Hampshire and the Highlands, Gina works full time in tech, and spends her evenings hunting down the best restaurants in the city.

Hoxton Mini Press is a small indie publisher based in east London. We make books with a dedication to good photography, passionate writing and lovely production. When we started the company people told us 'print was dead'. That inspired us. Books are no longer about information but objects in their own right: something to collect and own and inspire.

Want more opinion? Our pocket-sized, paperback *Opinionated Guides* to London will take you on a tour of the capital's best bits:

East London
London Architecture
Vegan London
London Green Spaces
Independent London
London Pubs
Sweet London
Kids' London

British Boutique Hotels: An Opinionated Guide
First edition, third printing

Published in 2021 by Hoxton Mini Press, London
Copyright © Hoxton Mini Press 2021. All rights reserved.

Text and photography by Gina Jackson*
Edited by Florence Filose
Design by Daniele Roa
Cover and map illustration by Charlotte Ager
Image retouching by Jarek Kotomski
Production by Anna De Pascale
Production and editorial support by Becca Jones

*Except for additional images credited on previous spread.

A CIP catalogue record for this book is available from the British Library.
The right of Gina Jackson to be identified as the creator of this Work
has been asserted under the Copyright, Designs and Patents Act 1988.

ISBN: 978-1-914314-03-2

Printed and bound by FINIDR, Czech Republic

Hoxton Mini Press is an environmentally conscious publisher,
committed to offsetting our carbon footprint. This book is 100% carbon
compensated, with offset purchased from Stand For Trees.

For every book you buy from our website, we plant a tree:
www.hoxtonminipress.com

FSC
www.fsc.org

MIX
Paper from
responsible sources
FSC® C014138